Brett Favre

Leader of the Pack

By Bill Gutman

MILLBROOK SPORTS WORLD
THE MILLBROOK PRESS
BROOKFIELD, CONNECTICUT

Allsport: cover (© Todd Rosenberg), pp. 25 (© Martin Venegas), 33
(© Otto Greule), 36 (© Brian Bahr), 38 (© Brian Bahr); NFL Photos: cover
inset (© Paul Jasienski), pp. 12 (© Perry McIntyre), 18 (© Bill Mount), 42
(© Jimmy Cribb), 46 (© Al Messerschmidt); Focus on Sports: pp. 3, 21
(© 1992 Chuck Solomon), 35, 41, 44 (© 1993 Tony Tomsic); AP/Wide World
Photos: pp. 4, 27, 28-29, 31, 43; © David Rae Morris, Impact Visuals: p. 8;
Vernon J. Biever: p. 16; Reuters/Lee Celano/Archive Photos: p. 39.

Library of Congress Cataloging-in-Publication Data
Gutman, Bill.
Brett Favre : leader of the pack / Bill Gutman.
p.   cm. — (Millbrook sports world)
Includes index.
Summary: A biography of the star quarterback, from his childhood in small-
town Mississippi, through his college days, to his professional career with
the Atlanta Falcons and Super Bowl champion Green Bay Packers.
ISBN 0-7613-0310-3 (lib. bdg.). — ISBN 0-7613-0328-6 (pbk.)
1. Favre, Brett—Juvenile literature.   2. Football players—United States—
Biography—Juvenile literature.   3. Green Bay Packers (Football team)—
Juvenile literature.   [1. Favre, Brett.   2. Football players.]   I. Title.
II. Series.
GV939.F29G88   1998
796.332′092—dc21
[B]   97-25905   CIP   AC

Published by The Millbrook Press, Inc.
2 Old New Milford Road
Brookfield, Connecticut   06804

BRETT
FAVRE

It was early in the second quarter of Super Bowl XXXI at the Louisiana Superdome in New Orleans on January 26, 1997. The momentum of the game had changed. Even though the heavily favored Green Bay Packers had taken an early, 10–0, lead over the New England Patriots and had seemed well on their way to victory, the Patriots had suddenly come alive. They scored twice in a little less than four minutes to take a 14–10 lead. The high-powered Green Bay offense seemed to fizzle. Quarterback Brett Favre and his teammates were having trouble moving the football against the stubborn New England defense.

Favre knew he had to light a fire under his team; he knew he had to motivate them. That was a job he had done well in the past. In fact, he had been named the National Football League's Most Valuable Player (MVP) the last two seasons, despite having to overcome a number of difficult setbacks.

A triumphant Brett Favre celebrates the final Green Bay points of the day as the Packers became Super Bowl champions with a 35–21 victory over the New England Patriots on January 26, 1997.

Now, in the second quarter of the Super Bowl, he found his team trailing and knew he had to do something about it. With less than a minute gone in the second quarter, Green Bay had the ball at their own 19-yard line.

Brett called a play and came to the line of scrimmage. Like most great quarterbacks, he looked over the defense and in a split second saw a weakness in the way the Patriots were lined up. The New England defensive backs were in single coverage against the Packers' three wide receivers. He saw that the Patriots' strong safety Lawyer Milloy was guarding the Packers' speedy Antonio Freeman.

Favre changed the play at the line of scrimmage, hollering out the new play to his teammates. He quickly called out a different blocking scheme that would give him the most protection from the Patriots' pass rushers. The new play would also send Antonio Freeman streaking down the right side of the field at full speed.

Favre called the signals and took the snap. He dropped back into the pocket, surrounded by his blockers. Then he looked downfield, spotted Freeman running behind his defender, and fired the football high and deep.

Freeman caught the ball in full stride and outran both Milloy and the Patriots' free safety Willie Clay to complete an electrifying 81-yard touchdown play. Not only was it the longest touchdown pass play in Super Bowl history, but it also put the Packers back in the lead. From there, the MVP quarterback, with help from kick returner Desmond Howard, defensive leader Reggie White, and the rest of the Packers, went on to win the game, 35–21, bringing the world championship back to Green Bay, Wisconsin.

For Brett Favre, it was the ultimate victory. But it wasn't one that had come easily. Brett had to deal with a series of personal problems as well as with the question of whether he could ever win the "big one." But as his team had gotten better, so had Brett. One of the toughest quarterbacks in the National Football League (NFL), he had played through a succession of painful injuries that would have benched many other signal callers.

But his dedication and unwillingness to come out of the lineup had nearly cost him his career and maybe even more. That's why his ultimate success was even more gratifying. Brett Favre had proved himself a winner both on and off the football field.

A KID WHO NEVER MISSED SCHOOL

Brett Lorenzo Favre (it rhymes with "carve") was born on October 10, 1969, in Gulfport, Mississippi. He was the second of four children born to Bonita and Irvin Favre. Scott was the oldest, followed by Brett, younger brother Jeff, and sister Brandi. The family moved to nearby Kiln, a small town of slightly more than seven thousand residents, where they lived at the end of a dirt road near a stretch of water called Rotten Bayou.

Both Mr. and Mrs. Favre were teachers. Bonita Favre taught special education, and Irvin Favre taught and coached football and baseball at Hancock North Central High School in Kiln for twenty-four years. It isn't surprising that sports always played a major part in their children's lives.

Brett grew up loving sports—football in particular. Two of his early idols were quarterbacks who played in the south—Archie Manning from the University of Mississippi and later the New Orleans Saints, and Roger Staubach of the Dallas Cowboys.

Brett began playing organized sports at Bay St. Louis Elementary School, and he always excelled. When he was in the sixth grade he already knew what he wanted to do with his life. He wrote a school essay saying that he was going to play professional football when he grew up.

When Brett was growing up in Kiln, Mississippi, his father, Irvin, was his football coach and his mother, Bonita, was there to patch up the bumps and bruises. They were also instrumental in young Brett not missing a single day of school from the third grade right through his high school graduation.

It's hard to say where Brett's toughness came from. Perhaps it was from his brothers competing with him in baseball, basketball, and football. Perhaps it was that his parents stressed responsibility and not letting down people who depended on him.

His toughness and strong will showed up clearly at school. For a period of ten years, Brett never missed a day of school—not a single day! His streak of perfect attendence ran from the time he was in the third grade until he graduated from high school. "My parents were teachers," he explained, "so it was tough to play hooky. Even if I was sick, I would tough it out and go to class."

When he wasn't in school, Brett could usually be found playing ball. From an early age he always had a very strong throwing arm. At first, he seemed to showcase it more on the baseball diamond. When he was in the eighth grade, he was good enough to become the starting third baseman on the Hancock North Central High School team.

He could also hit. As an eighth grader, he led the team in hitting with a .325 batting average. In fact, he would lead the team in hitting for five straight years, right through his senior year.

But by the time he was in high school, football had become his real love. Yet in spite of Brett's obvious talent for throwing the football, the coach, Brett's father, Irvin Favre, favored what was called the wishbone offense at Hancock North Central.

In the wishbone the quarterback simply didn't throw the ball very often. He did more running and blocking than passing. Asked later why he hadn't let Brett showcase his strong throwing arm more often, Irvin Favre answered as a football coach, not as a father: "Because we had a kid who was a 1,000-yard rusher, and we kept winning with what we were doing," he said.

Because he hadn't had a chance to show off his throwing, Brett had little hope of becoming a passing quarterback at a major college when he began playing his senior season at Hancock North Central in 1986. As for the NFL, that was beginning to look like a distant dream.

BECOMING A GOLDEN EAGLE

By most standards, Brett had a fine career at Hancock North Central High. He played quarterback on offense and strong safety on defense. He also handled all the kicking chores, punting and placekicking. After his senior season ended, he played in the Mississippi high school all-star game.

But he still didn't know what college held for him. In fact, for a while, he wondered if he'd be going as a student only. "I was never recruited for college," he said. "No one really wanted me. Coming from Kiln, playing for a small school and not really putting up big numbers, well, nobody knows who you are."

But one Division-I school took an interest. Coaches from the University of Southern Mississippi in nearby Hattiesburg came to take a look at him. Brett's father had attended Southern Miss and pitched on the baseball team.

The coaches at Southern Miss saw a kid who was 6 feet 2 inches (188 centimeters), and already weighed more than 200 pounds (91 kilograms). He had good speed and wasn't afraid to hit or be hit. They projected him as a defensive back and gave him a scholarship with the idea that he could become an outstanding safety. But Brett had other ideas. When the football team, the Golden Eagles, held its first practice in the fall of 1987, he asked to work out at both safety and quarterback.

Brett knew that didn't mean instant success. Even though he was working out at quarterback, his name was seventh on the depth chart. There were six other quarterbacks ahead of him. But that didn't deter him. "I've always had to struggle for what I've got," Brett would say later. "I was always the underdog."

Never one to duck a tough fight, Brett continued to work hard at quarterback. By the time the 1987 season was about to open, he had moved up to number three on the depth chart.

The coaches saw that he had the strongest throwing arm among the quarterbacks and was a fierce competitor who never quit. He was also a natural leader who urged those around him to give 100 percent. He didn't play in the opening game. But in the Golden Eagles' second game against Tulane University, Southern Miss trailed at the half and the offense wasn't moving the ball. Suddenly, the coaches made a decision. Freshman quarterback Brett Favre was in the lineup.

After a couple of plays to calm himself from the excitement of quarterbacking a college team, Brett settled down. He began to put life into the Golden Eagles' offense. Using his strong arm, he started connecting with his receivers. When the game ended, Brett had thrown for a pair of touchdowns and led his club to a 31–24, come-from-behind victory.

Brett was thrown into big-time college football with little experience as a drop-back passing quarterback. When he came in to lead his team to a victory over Tulane, he was still 17 years old. He knew he had a lot to learn. He also knew there would be failures to go along with his successes.

Several weeks later he began to show his coaches and teammates that he was the best person for the job of starting quarterback. Playing against Southwestern Louisiana, he completed 21 of 39 passes for a school record 295 yards. Against both East Carolina and Louisville, he fired three touchdown passes. He was still a raw talent, sometimes undisciplined, occasionally out of control. But when he was on his game, his passing arm could eat up the yardage and lead to rapid offensive explosions.

When the season ended, Brett had completed 79 of 194 passes for 1,264 yards and a school record 14 touchdowns. His completion percentage was just 40.7, however, and he had thrown 13 interceptions. But overall it had been a successful season and gave him reason to believe his NFL dream *was* still alive.

A TOP COLLEGIATE QUARTERBACK

Brett was a much more confident quarterback when he returned for the 1988 season. It didn't take long for him to show it on the field. The Golden Eagles had a new coach, Curley Hallman, who built his high-powered offense around the strong-armed sophomore quarterback. The team began winning, and Brett began putting up big-time numbers.

Against East Carolina, he completed 20 of 32 passes for 301 yards, the first 300-yard passing game in school history. He completed another 20 of 32 against Louisville for 275 yards and 19 of 36 versus Memphis State for 241 yards. He threw for three touchdowns in games against Virginia Tech, Tulane, and Southwestern Louisiana. And this season, he was throwing to his receivers, not to the other team. He finished the season with a streak of 144 passes without a single interception.

Brett and his teammates at Southern Miss always played with a purpose. One thing they loved was upsetting big-name schools. "Southern Miss was a

place where everyone had been rejected by the big schools for some reason," Brett explained. "We were the Island of Misfits. We thrived on that. We'd play Alabama, Auburn—schools like that—and there would always be stories in the papers about how we'd been rejected by them. Whenever we'd come out and win the game, guys would be yelling on the field, 'What's wrong with us now?' It was a great way to play."

The Golden Eagles finished the regular 1988 season with a 9–2 record, then went out and whipped the University of Texas at El Paso, 38–18, in the Independence Bowl. Brett connected on 15 of 26 passes for 157 yards and a score in the final game of the season. It had indeed been a great year for him.

He had completed 178 of 319 passes for 2,271 yards, and had 16 touchdowns with only five interceptions in 1988. He set a slew of school records, including those for number of touchdown passes, passing yards, and total offense (2,256 yards). After the season he was named the Independence Bowl Association Offensive Player of the Year and also named to the first team of the All-Metro Conference.

Before his junior season of 1989, Brett finally began getting press notices outside of Mississippi. Many preseason college football analysts were now including him among the top college quarterbacks in the country. It was exciting to Brett that he and the team might get some national publicity.

"A writer came down to Southern Miss to do an article for *Sports Illustrated*," Brett said. "He said he wasn't sure the article would be in, but if we beat Florida State in our opener, he was pretty sure it would make it. So we went out and pulled the upset. All I'm thinking about the last few minutes on the field is, 'God, I'm going to be in *Sports Illustrated*.'"

At Southern Mississippi, Brett made his mark as a strong-armed quarterback who loved to upset nationally ranked teams.

The article never appeared, even though Brett had been brilliant in the game, throwing for 282 yards and two touchdowns as the Golden Eagles upset the nationally ranked Florida State Seminoles, 30–26. His great effort did lead to him being named United Press International (UPI) Offensive Player of the Week, however.

It was a great victory and set the stage for a productive season. In the ensuing weeks, Brett proved himself one of the top passers in the country, with an arm so strong that it seemed he could strike from anywhere.

He threw for a Southern Mississippi record 345 yards against Memphis State, for 303 yards against Texas A&M, and 300 yards more against nationally ranked Alabama. In a game against East Carolina, he completed 26 of 35 passes for an amazing 74.3 completion percentage. Brett finished his junior year with 206 completions in 381 tries, for 2,588 yards, 14 touchdowns, and just ten interceptions.

Yet he still wasn't mentioned on any of the postseason All-America teams. A number of NFL scouts had already seen him, however, and had given his throwing arm high grades. Most of them felt he had NFL potential, but wanted to see a solid senior year before deciding how good he might be.

Brett, too, left school that year looking forward to the upcoming 1990 season. He was a special education major at Southern Miss and now projected as a possible All-American. He returned home to Kiln for the summer to be with his family and to have some fun. Then, in July, something happened that might have not only cost Brett his football career but his life as well.

A CLOSE CALL

Late on the hot Mississippi afternoon of July 14, 1990, Brett was returning home from a day of fun and sun at a place called Ship Island. Driving his Nissan Maxima, he was just a mile from home when he said he was blinded by the lights of another car. He swerved to avoid a collision. His car hit some loose gravel, flipped into the air, and rolled several times. Brett's brother Scott was driving behind him and saw the whole thing. He said the car flipped so high "you could have driven a dump truck underneath."

Scott had to break the front window with a golf club so he could pull Brett from the twisted wreckage. He could see his brother was badly hurt. At the hospital the doctors told the Favres that Brett had a concussion, lacerations, and a cracked vertebra. But they said that since he was young and strong, he should be all right in a short time.

Sure enough, Brett was out of the hospital after a short time and back home. He began to think about football again. But he soon realized that something more was wrong with him.

"At first I thought I was okay," Brett said. "But I wasn't eating much, and when I did, I was throwing up. Then I started having abdominal pains, and they began getting worse. I went back to the hospital and they found that I had a major intestinal problem."

Doctors had to perform immediate surgery. On August 7 they removed some 30 inches (76 centimeters) of intestine that had been damaged in the accident, telling him that with rest he would be fine. But it was a major setback for a football player who hoped to be ready for the start of the most important season of his life.

When he finally returned to school he was some 30 pounds (14 kilograms) underweight. Doctors told him he would likely miss the first four games.

What very few people fully realized then was the strong will and toughness of Brett Favre. He watched his teammates play their opener in 1990, then announced that he intended to play in the second game against powerful Alabama. It was scheduled for September 8, just a month after his surgery. Coach Hallman checked with the doctors, who gave Brett the green light.

As a young quarterback with the Packers, Brett had a youthful but determined look. It was this same determination that drove him in his senior year at Southern Miss. Though seriously injured in a summer auto accident, Brett returned in the second game of the season and led his team to a 27–24 upset of powerful Alabama.

Though not at full strength, Brett had lost nothing in the leadership department. He played well within himself, controlling the offense and keeping the Alabama defense on the field as much as possible. When it ended, Southern Miss had a significant, 27–24, upset victory.

"You can call it a miracle or a legend or whatever ..." said Alabama coach Gene Stallings. "I just know that on that day, Brett Favre was larger than life."

Later in the season, Brett would engineer yet another upset, a 13–12 victory over nationally ranked Auburn. That turned out to be his best game yet, as he threw for 207 yards and two scores. But despite this, it hadn't been the kind of senior year everyone, including Brett, had envisioned. Brett never quite regained all his strength. As a result, his numbers were down.

The team finished at 8–4, including a loss to North Carolina State in the postseason All-American Bowl. Brett had connected on 150 of 275 passes for 1,572 yards, good for a 54.5 completion percentage. His touchdown passes were down to seven against six interceptions. Those numbers didn't show the real Brett Favre.

His Southern Mississippi career had seen him set some 15 school records, both season and career, all for passing and total offense. After the season ended, he became a hot item with NFL scouts when he was named the Most Valuable Player in the postseason East-West Shrine game.

One scout who saw what he liked at the Shrine game was Ron Wolf, at that time working for the New York Jets. Wolf saw a quarterback who not only threw the ball well, but seemed to have that quality of leadership that made his team-mates respond to him.

"I just really liked him," Wolf said, when confronted by those who didn't think Brett was a top NFL prospect. "He had that unexplainable something about him."

With the NFL draft approaching, Brett hadn't wavered in his desire to be a pro quarterback. Then he learned of the New York Jets' big interest in him. But the Jets never got a chance—the Atlanta Falcons, picking right before the Jets, took Brett with their second-round pick. He was the thirty-third pick in the draft, the third quarterback chosen. To Brett, it didn't matter. He was going to be in the National Football League. In addition, the Falcons, under colorful coach Jerry Glanville, were considered a play-off contender for the 1991 season.

However, he had come in as the number-three quarterback behind starter Chris Miller and backup Billy Joe Tolliver. And while he looked pretty good in the preseason, the regular season turned into a bitter disappointment.

Though the Falcons finished at 10–6 and made the play-offs in 1991, Brett wasn't really part of it. As the third-string quarterback, he was only active for three of the team's 16 games. He got into parts of two games as a mop-up and failed to complete a pass in five tries.

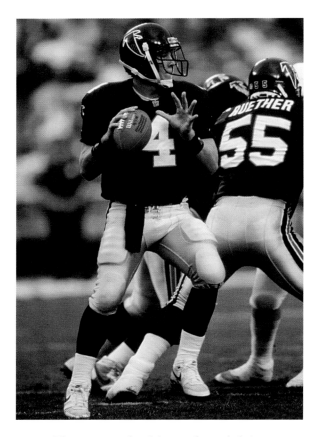

This is a sight Atlanta fans didn't see very often. Though Brett was drafted by the Atlanta Falcons in 1991, he was active for only three games and failed to complete a pass in five attempts.

"The number-three guy gets virtually no snaps during practice," Irvin Favre said. "[The situation] left Brett really depressed, and it wound up affecting his work habits."

Because he was depressed about not playing, Brett ended up in Coach Glanville's doghouse. Glanville said that Brett was "uncoachable." Brett began to feel that there wasn't much future for him in Atlanta.

Behind the scenes, however, Brett's name had become prominent in talks between the Falcons and the Green Bay Packers. The Packers had a new general manager in Ron Wolf—the same Ron Wolf who had scouted for the Jets and had wanted Brett for that team. The Packers also had a new head coach, Mike Holmgren, who had seen Brett work out after his senior year at Southern Miss. Holmgren liked Brett's arm strength and his self-confidence.

Looking to rebuild the Packers, Wolf and Holmgren worked out a trade. On February 10, 1992, it was announced that Brett Favre had been dealt to the Packers in exchange for Green Bay's number-one draft choice in 1992.

TO THE FROZEN FIELDS OF GREEN BAY

In 1992, Brett was not only going to a new team but to a whole new environment. Green Bay was in Wisconsin, where the winters were frigid. Warm-weather teams from the South and West often found the harsh weather conditions at frozen Lambeau Field difficult to withstand.

He was also going to a team with a long and glorious tradition that was begging for a revival. The golden era of the Packers had begun in 1959 when the legendary coach Vince Lombardi took over the team. With Lombardi driving them, the Packers built a dynasty, winning NFL titles in 1961, 1962, 1965, 1966, and 1967. Following the 1966 and 1967 seasons, the Packers won the first two Super Bowls ever played.

But after Lombardi's retirement following the second Super Bowl, things were never the same. From 1968 to 1991, the Packers had racked up just five winning seasons and no championships. In 1991, Brett's rookie year with the Falcons, the Packers finished with a terrible 4–12 record. That's when the team hired Mike Holmgren as its new coach and looked to rebuild.

Coach Holmgren was known as an offensive specialist. His playbook contained more than a thousand plays, and his passing scheme was not easy to master. As soon as he arrived in Green Bay, Brett went about learning the offense. It wasn't easy, and sometime later, he would say, "In the first year or so I don't think anybody on our team knew exactly what we were doing."

The returning starter at quarterback in 1992 was Don Majkowski, who had put together a fine season in 1989. But Majkowski also had a history of injuries. He had missed fourteen full games and parts of five others in 1990 and 1991. Now, the coaches weren't sure what to do with him.

Majkowski started the first two games of the season, both of which the Packers lost. Then in game three, against the Cincinnati Bengals, Majkowski went down in the first quarter with strained ankle ligaments. Suddenly, less than a month before his twenty-third birthday, Brett Favre was quarterbacking the Green Bay Packers.

He started with a bang. Relieving Majkowski, Brett completed 22 of 39 passes for 289 yards and two scores. But the numbers weren't the whole story. It was Brett's 35-yard touchdown pass to wide receiver Kitrick Taylor with just 13 seconds left that made the headlines. The touchdown and extra point gave the Packers a 24–23 victory. Green Bay fans roared with delight. They felt they had just seen the future. But Brett himself wasn't so sure. "What people don't re-member about that day is that I should have had six or seven interceptions," he would admit. "I was all over the place."

A week later Brett completed 14 of 19 passes for 210 yards and another two touchdowns as the Pack whipped the Pittsburgh Steelers. Coach Holmgren had seen enough. He named Brett the starting quarterback for the remainder of the season.

Though the Packers lost their next three games, they finished things out by winning seven of their last nine, including six in a row. That gave the team a 9–7 record, their best in 20 years. They didn't make the play-offs, but it looked as if they had found a quarterback.

During the year Brett also showed the toughness that was becoming his trademark. In a game against the Philadelphia Eagles, he suffered a separated left shoulder after a hard hit by defensive end Reggie White. Most quarterbacks would have left the game. Brett Favre didn't.

Traded to Green Bay in 1992, Brett became the starting quarterback when veteran Don Majkowski was injured. Soon, Packer fans were used to seeing number 4 dropping back and firing the ball downfield with his rifle arm.

Despite the fact that he couldn't lift his arm as high as his shoulder and couldn't hand off to the left, he continued to play. Once again he led his team to a come-from-behind 27–24 victory. Even with the painful injury, Brett completed 23 of 33 passes for 275 yards and two scores.

Brett started the final thirteen games of 1992. He completed 302 of 471 passes for a 64.1 percentage and 3,227 yards. He had 18 touchdown passes against 13 interceptions. His completion percentage broke the Green Bay record of 63.74 set by the great Bart Starr.

At the close of the regular season, Brett became the youngest quarterback ever to play in the Pro Bowl, the annual all-star game that pits the National Football Conference (NFC) against the American Football Conference (AFC). All this happened just a year after his disappointing rookie season when he was banished from Atlanta with his NFL future in doubt.

A CRISIS IN CONFIDENCE

The Packers continued to build. Prior to the 1993 season, the team took a big step toward upgrading the defense. They signed free agent Reggie White, already known as one of the greatest defensive ends ever. He was the Philadelphia Eagles player who had separated Brett's shoulder the year before.

By most standards, the Packers were a very good team in 1993. Superstar wide receiver Sterling Sharpe caught a record 112 passes. White tied for the most quarterback sacks in the NFC with 13. And Brett Favre threw for 3,303 yards with 19 touchdown passes. Once again, the Pack finished at 9–7. Only this time they made it to the play-offs.

In the first round, the Pack whipped the Detroit Lions, 28–24. Brett threw a spectacular touchdown pass to Sharpe with just fifty-five seconds left to win the game. But the bubble burst a week later when the Packers lost, 27–17, to the eventual Super Bowl champion, the Dallas Cowboys.

To outsiders, it seemed like it had been a successful season. But behind the scenes, there was a growing problem between head coach Holmgren and his young quarterback.

In the coach's opinion, Brett had not made progress in 1993. True, he had thrown 19 touchdown passes. But he was also intercepted 24 times. That was not like Brett. His final quarterback rating had dropped from 85.3 in 1992 to 72.2 in 1993. The coach felt that Brett wasn't playing within the system.

When 1994 rolled around, everyone wondered if the Packers could advance to that next level and be among the NFL's elite teams. But after seven games they were at a disappointing 3–4.

Before the season started, Coach Holmgren had told Brett, "I will not hesitate to pull you if we're losing games with the same mistakes we made last year."

In the seventh game against the Minnesota Vikings, Brett bruised a hip and was replaced by backup quarterback Mark Brunell. The Packers lost in overtime, 13–10. All that week Holmgren and his coaches talked about the possibility of benching Brett and making Brunell the starting quarterback. But the head coach also felt that Brett was very close to finally mastering his complicated offense. Finally, he called Brett into his office.

"Buddy, it's your job," he told him. "We're joined at the hip. Either we're going to the Super Bowl together, or we're going down together."

That feeling was shared by Packers quarterback coach Steve Marucci. When he saw Brett after the meeting with Holmgren he gave the quarterback a pep talk. He told him he could sulk or pick himself up and be a winner.

Brett looked Marucci in the eye and said, "The second half of the season is going to be like no other."

Confident that the job of quarterback was still his, Brett began playing the best football of his life. The Pack won their next three games, and then after a

three-game losing streak, won their next four. Brett had one big game after another. He had four touchdown passes with no interceptions against the Cowboys, threw for 366 yards with three scores against the Detroit Lions, and passed
for 321 yards with a pair of touchdowns against the Falcons.

It was only after he had turned things around that Brett admitted how difficult it had been for him. "I struggled and I struggled for a long time," he said.
"But think about it. I got thrown into the toughest offense in the game as a starter
at twenty-two. Every other guy who's played it sat for a year or two and learned.
Joe Montana sat behind Steve DeBerg. Steve Young sat behind Montana. That's
why it was frustrating when people would get on me."

The strong finish put the Packers at 9–7 for the season. But the team suffered a huge loss late in the year when Sterling Sharpe was sidelined with a neck
injury that not only would keep him out of the play-offs, but would also end his
career. Brett lost his top receiver—one of the great pass catchers in the league.

Yet Brett managed to have an outstanding season. He finished the regular
campaign with 363 completions out of 582 tries for 3,882 big yards. He had
thrown for a team record 33 touchdowns, second in the league only to Steve
Young's 35, and had just 14 passes intercepted. His 90.7 quarterback rating was
second best, behind Young.

In a sense, the play-offs were a copy of the year before. In the first round,
the Pack defeated the Lions once more, this time by a 16–12 count. Next for the
Packers was the defending Super Bowl champion Cowboys. But once again the
Cowboys were too strong, defeating the Packers in Texas, 35–9. As one writer
put it, "With no running game to rely upon and no Sterling Sharpe to throw to,
Brett Favre had no chance against the surging Dallas defense."

*By the end of the 1994 season, Brett was
putting up big numbers. He was also taking
some big hits, like this one against the
Cowboys, showing that he was one of the
toughest quarterbacks in the league.*

It was true. But at the same time, 1994 had been a turning point. Many Packer fans felt it was just a matter of time before Coach Holmgren, Brett, and Reggie White led the Packers back to the top.

MOST VALUABLE PLAYER

At the beginning of the 1995 season Brett Favre was just 25 years old. But he was already entering his fourth season as the Packers' starting quarterback. And judging by the way he played during the second half of 1994, he was on the brink of becoming a superstar.

This time, the Packers got off to a good start, winning five of their first seven games. Brett was playing better than ever. Against the Chicago Bears in game two, Brett completed a team record 99-yard touchdown bomb to wide receiver Robert Brooks. It was only the eighth time in NFL history that a quarterback had thrown a touchdown pass that long.

The numbers kept coming. Against Detroit, Brett threw for 342 yards. A week later in a game with Minnesota, the rifle-armed quarterback struck for four touchdown passes. Defenses were trying everything to stop him, and Brett was getting banged up week after week. But he wouldn't sit down. His reputation as the toughest quarterback in the league was growing.

Then came the ninth game of the season, at Minnesota on November 5. Brett already had assorted aches and pains, including a throbbing toe, bruised right shoulder, arthritic right hip, bruised left knee, and sore lower back. Late in the second quarter Brett was hit hard by several Vikings defenders. He got up hobbling, his left ankle severely sprained. It was yet another painful injury on top of the others.

Brett reluctantly sat out the remainder of the first half and tried to play in the second half, but he couldn't do it. Some felt that he might be out a few weeks while the ankle healed. But a week later he was back against the Chicago Bears,

Prior to the 1995 season, Brett (second from left) appeared with fellow quarterbacks Jim Kelly (left), Dan Marino (second from right), and Drew Bledsoe as part of the Cadillac NFL Golf Classic to benefit the Tomorrow's Children Fund.

completing 25 of 33 passes for 336 yards. He also tied a team record with five touchdown passes that day. For his efforts, he was named NFL Offensive Player of the Week.

With Brett continuing to play brilliantly, the Packers won seven of their remaining nine games to take the NFC Central Division title with an 11–5 record. It was the Pack's first divisional title since 1972. There were a number of outstanding players on the team now, but no one's star shone as brightly as Brett's.

For the season, he completed 359 of 570 passes for a league best 4,413 yards and a 63.0 percentage. He also led the NFL with 38 touchdown passes, the third-highest total in league history. And he had had just 13 throws intercepted. His quarterback rating of 99.5 was a career best and second in the NFL.

There was more. During the season, Brett had also thrown his one hundredth career touchdown pass. He had done it in just sixty-two games. Only Dan Marino and the legendary Johnny Unitas had done it faster, Marino in forty-four games and Unitas in fifty-three.

But that still wasn't all. Brett was named the starting quarterback for the NFC in the postseason Pro Bowl; Offensive Player of the Year by the Associated Press (AP); and quarterback of the All-Pro Team. And to top it off, he was named the National Football

During the 1995 season, Brett tossed his 100th career touchdown pass. He could throw from the pocket, or on the run as he is doing here against Detroit. When the season ended, he was named the NFL's Most Valuable Player.

League's Most Valuable Player by the AP. He was the first Packer to win the MVP prize since Bart Starr had done so back in 1966. The awards and praise were great, but one thing was more important. "Our goal is to win the Super Bowl," Brett said. "Everything else is secondary."

The team's first play-off game was at home at Lambeau Field against the Atlanta Falcons. Brett picked his former team apart, completing 24 of 35 passes for 199 yards and three touchdowns. The Packers led 27–10 at the half and went on to an easy, 37–20, victory. Next, they would have to face the defending Super Bowl champion San Francisco 49ers.

To show the confidence the Packers now had in their leader, safety LeRoy Butler was asked to name three reasons why he felt that his team could beat the 49ers. Butler didn't have to think twice about his answer. "Brett, Brett, Brett," he said quickly.

When told of Butler's answer, Brett replied, "That's great. To me as a player that's what you want them to say, that we're putting it all on Brett."

Despite being the visiting team at San Francisco, Brett and the Packers showed they were ready to take on the best in the league. With their quarterback hitting on 21 of 28 passes for 299 yards and two scores, the Pack beat the Niners, 27–17, to advance to the NFC championship game against their old nemesis, the Dallas Cowboys. The club was now just a step away from going to the Super Bowl.

The Packers had lost to Dallas in the play-offs the last two years. This time they felt it would be different. "Each time we went down there we didn't feel we belonged in that building with them," Brett said. "Now we do."

The Packers kept the game close. Dallas had a 24–17 lead at the half despite a pair of Favre touchdown passes. A brilliant touchdown toss to Robert Brooks midway through the third period gave Green Bay a 27–24 lead. After the

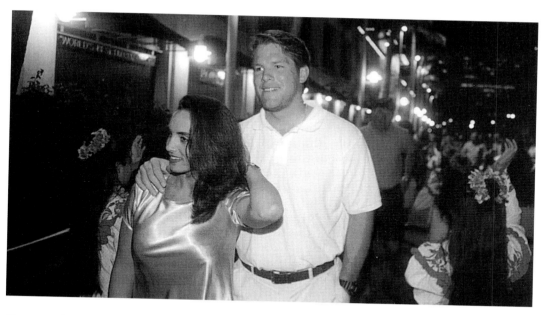

Brett and longtime girlfriend Deanna Tynes arrive at the Pro Bowl party in January 1996 in Honolulu. Brett was the starting quarterback for the NFC. Later in the year, he and Deanna were married.

Cowboys regained the lead at 31–27, Brett threw a key interception. Dallas then drove for the touchdown that put the game on ice. The final score was 38–27. Green Bay had come close, but lost once again to the Cowboys.

Brett had completed 21 passes in 39 tries for 307 yards and three touchdowns. But two interceptions hurt him. Reggie White remembered Brett's reaction as the Packers returned home. "Going home on the airplane Brett had tears in his eyes," White said. "He made me a promise that he would lead the team to the Super Bowl next year."

But before he could attempt that, Brett Favre would have to face the biggest crisis of his life.

THE PRICE OF PAIN

It is not unusual for professional football players to play while injured or in pain. Many times they will use painkilling drugs to help them through a game. Brett was no exception. He first used a painkiller in 1992, when he separated his shoulder in a game against the Eagles. That was the year he won the quarterback job and didn't want to lose it by sitting out.

Later, Brett began taking a prescription drug called Vicodin. It is a powerful narcotic-analgesic painkiller. As his injuries mounted during his MVP season of 1995, he began using Vicodin more and more. And he continued to play the best football of his life.

After the season Brett went into the hospital for surgery on the ankle he had injured against Minnesota. He had started 68 straight games as quarterback. It was the longest starting streak among all NFL quarterbacks. Yet he was undergoing his fifth operation in six years.

While still in the hospital, he had an unexpected seizure. When he came to, one of the team doctors told him what had happened. "You've just suffered a seizure," the doctor said. "People can die from those."

It was then that Brett began thinking that the Vicodin may have helped cause the seizure. He had been taking more of the pills than anyone knew, getting them from teammates and exceeding the number that the doctors prescribed. The more he thought about it, the more he realized he had come to depend on the pills. He knew that he had to stop.

On May 14, 1996, Brett held a news conference. He announced that he had a dependency on painkillers and was entering the Menninger Clinic, a rehabilitation center in Topeka, Kansas.

"I quit cold turkey," Brett said, adding that he hadn't taken Vicodin since the seizure. He felt that his action could help others. "I'm sure there are a ton of

NFL players out there—I mean it, a ton—who'll watch me come out and say to themselves, 'Man, that's me.' That's one reason I'm talking. I hope I can help some players get help. I realize now how dangerous it is to keep using these [drugs]."

Brett said part of the reason for his taking so many pills was simply to keep playing. He felt he owed it to the team. And he also didn't want to lose his job to injury. "Then it just got out of hand," he added.

He also told people that being a professional athlete isn't always what it's made out to be. "I'm twenty-six years old," he said. "I just threw 38 touchdown passes in one year, and I'm the NFL MVP. People look at me and say, 'I'd love to be that guy.' But if they knew what it took to be that guy, they wouldn't love to be him, I can guarantee you that."

Brett turned his stay at the clinic into a positive time in more ways than one. He worked out regularly and did a lot of run-

It was constant, punishing hits like this one that contributed to Brett's addiction to painkillers. In May 1996, he entered the Menninger Clinic in Kansas, where he said he quit the drugs "cold turkey." He then decided to talk about his addiction in order to help others.

ning. When he left the clinic after a forty-five day stay, he was in the best physical shape of his life. His playing weight had dropped from 230 to 218 pounds (104 to 99 kilograms). And his body fat was down from 18 percent to a mere 8 percent. While he was glad to be free of Vicodin and hopeful he had helped other players by his example, there was one thing that bothered him.

Brett fully realized he had a serious problem. But he wanted it made clear that what happened to him wasn't the same as what happens to someone who decides on his own to take drugs. Brett didn't want to be put in the same class as someone who voluntarily begins using recreational drugs such as marijuana and cocaine and becomes dependent on them. His problem came from a medication prescribed by doctors to help him with pain, and it got the best of him. Hopefully, the addiction was now behind Brett forever.

A PROMISE KEPT

In the eyes of many, the team to beat in 1996 was the Green Bay Packers. The Pack was now strong on both offense and defense, with many outstanding individual players. Of course, the one player they could least afford to lose was Brett Favre.

Brett came into the season prepared to deal with the aches and pains of being an NFL quarterback in a new way. He would only take nonprescription, over-the-counter medications, such as Motrin, to help his pains. He also found that exercising regularly kept his body in better shape than resting it. "If I take a day off, the pain comes back," he said. He constantly worked out with weights or on a stationary bike or treadmill. Nagging injuries were part of the game, and Brett would do his best to overcome them. Once again he would start all 16 regular-season games, and once again he would be the best quarterback in the league.

Brett and his teammates set the tone for the season in the opener against the Buccaneers at Tampa Bay. They won the game easily, 34–3, as Brett completed 20 of 27 passes for 247 yards and four touchdowns. His first week out in

1996, he was named NFC Offensive Player of the Week. Brett and the Pack were off and running.

The Packers won their first three and eight of their first nine games. With an 8–1 mark the team was obviously at or near the top of the league. Then they faltered with a 27–20 loss to the Kansas City Chiefs and a 21–6 defeat at the hands of archrival Dallas. Two more wins followed, and on December 8 the Pack hosted the Denver Broncos at Lambeau Field. Green Bay was at 10–3, while the Broncos had a 12–1 record. Brett and his teammates felt it was time to make a statement.

A cool and confident Brett directed the Green Bay offense like a seasoned veteran in 1996. By mid-season, the Packers looked like the best team in the league and became early favorites to win the Super Bowl.

Although he grew up in the Deep South, Brett loved playing at frozen Lambeau Field in Green Bay in winter. He led the 1996 Pack to a 13–3 record and division title. He was an All-Pro and named the NFL's Most Valuable Player for a second straight year.

Green Bay spoke loud, beating Denver, 41–6. Brett told his teammates to play hard all the way. "I told them to pour it on all through the second half," he said, "because I wanted to make a statement. It wasn't so much directed at Denver . . . I wanted other teams to see what we can do when we have our house in order."

Against Denver, Brett completed 20 of 38 passes for 280 yards and four touchdowns. After that, the Packers wouldn't lose again. They finished the regular season with a 13–3 mark, the best in the NFC. It had been an incredible year so far. Players like Reggie White, Antonio Freeman, fullback Dorsey Levens, kick returner Desmond Howard, and others were all outstanding. But no one had a better season than Brett Favre.

Brett completed 325 of 543 passes for 3,899 yards and a league-leading 39 touchdowns. He had just 13 interceptions and finished with a quarterback rating of 95.6. In just five seasons he had thrown 147 touchdown passes, second in Packers history to Bart Starr's 152.

Over the prior three years, Brett had thrown for 110 touchdowns. At a distant second was Dan Marino with 71. Brett also had the best pass-to-interception ratio in the league over that time. He was named first team All-Pro once again, and won a slew of postseason honors. But the most important was a second straight Most Valuable Player prize from the AP. The only other player ever to win the MVP two years in a row was Joe Montana, the former San Francisco quarterback great.

Now, praise for Brett came from everywhere—his teammates, opponents, fans, and former players. Former NFL coach and current announcer John Madden said that Brett "plays quarterback like a nose tackle. He has so much adrenalin flowing that even he says, 'I don't know where the first five passes are going to go.'"

Others said the more you hit him, the better he got. But perhaps the ultimate compliment came from former Packers great Bart Starr, who had quarterbacked all those title teams in the Coach Lombardi era. "He's just a sensational young quarterback," Starr said. "I love watching him play. He has grown to execute a system expertly. He's extremely talented and I love his courage. His mobility, the ability to move and throw on the run, his arm strength enables him to eat teams alive. I have never seen a quarterback in this league at his young age as good as he is."

But there was still one piece of unfinished business—the play-offs. In the first round the Pack played host to the still tough San Francisco 49ers. On a wet, muddy field the Packers played grind-it-out football and won easily, 35–14.

Next came the NFC championship game. The Packers were hoping to go up against their old nemesis, the Dallas Cowboys. But they would be up against the Carolina Panthers, a two-year-old expansion team, already among the league's elite, who had upset the Cowboys.

As usual, Brett was so pumped up that some of the early passes went awry. One was picked off by linebacker Sam Mills, who took it back to the two-yard line, setting up a Carolina touchdown. The Pack trailed, 7–0.

But Brett kept his cool. On the first play of the second quarter he tied the game by lofting a 29-yard touchdown pass to running back Dorsey Levens. Carolina hit on a field goal to take a 10–7 lead. But after that, it was all Green Bay. Brett played brilliantly, and the Packers rolled to a 30–13 victory. He had hit on 19 of 29 passes for 292 yards and two scores. Finally, the Packers were returning to the Super Bowl after twenty-nine years.

After the game Brett hugged veteran defensive end Reggie White, who had never won a title of any kind since he began playing football. "Congratulations," he said. "You deserve this."

The two tough men embraced and the tears flowed. Later, Brett

Brett (center) and two of his Packer teammates celebrate their first round, 35–14, play-off victory over the San Francisco 49ers.

talked about what going to the Super Bowl meant. "We've had to overcome so many obstacles," he said, "and I think people were moved by our quest. This team has been kind of like potluck, a mixture of the good, the bad, and the ugly. I've done a lot of thinking, crying, cheering, and hugging over the past year, and it all began that day in Dallas."

Brett was talking about the 38–27 loss to Dallas in the NFC title game the year before. That's when he made a promise to his team to get them to the Super Bowl. Now, he could say that he had kept it.

SUPER AT LAST

The excitement ran high before the Packers met the New England Patriots at the Louisiana Superdome in Super Bowl XXXI. Playing in New Orleans made it

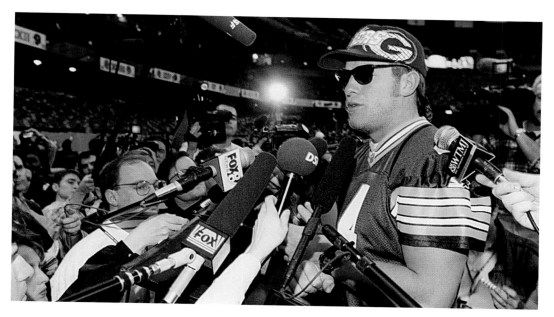

Brett was center of attention in New Orleans prior to Super Bowl XXXI. After all, he was returning to the South to try to lead the Packers to the championship. By this time, he was used to having a bevy of microphones thrust in his face.

extra special for Brett. His home in Kiln was only about 50 miles (80 kilometers) away.

Though the Patriots had a fine young quarterback in Drew Bledsoe, many felt that the difference in the game would be Brett. One of those was Kerry Collins, the second-year quarterback of the Carolina Panthers. "Brett Favre is as good a quarterback as has been around in a long time," Collins said. "He's a very heady quarterback and he makes big plays. [The Packers'] defense is similar to the 49ers', but Brett just takes them to another level."

Those big plays started on just the second snap of the game. The Packers had the ball at their own 46-yard line. Brett saw that New England's defense meant to blitz. He changed the play at the line of scrimmage, dropped back quickly, and fired deep. Wideout Andre Rison caught the ball behind the New England defense and waltzed into the end zone to complete a 54-yard touchdown.

After the Patriots had come back to take a 14–10 lead, Brett threw the brilliant 81-yard touchdown pass to Antonio Freeman to put his team in front again. Then he led the Pack to a 27–14 half-time lead.

After the Patriots had closed it to 27–21 late in the third period, Desmond Howard put the game to bed with a 99-yard kickoff return for the final score of the game. Then the Green Bay defense took over—Reggie White sacked Drew Bledsoe twice in a row. The Packers won it, 35–21. They were Super Bowl champions at last.

Desmond Howard was named the Super Bowl MVP for his record 244 yards on kickoff and punt returns. But Brett Favre and Reggie White—the two team leaders—had also been brilliant. Brett completed 14 of 27 passes for 246 yards and two big scores. White had three sacks and was a demon on defense all afternoon.

After the game Brett reflected on the entire year. It had been a year in which he had to undergo rehabilitation for his addiction to Vicodin. It had been a year in which he had seen the death of his best friend from home, who had been killed in a car accident, in which Brett's brother Scott had been driving. And it was a year in which he had promised his team a Super Bowl victory.

"Through everything," he said, "I really believed I'd be here today . . . talking about being world champions. My best friend's gone forever. Trouble never seems to be far away, and the future won't all be rosy. But they can't take this away from me.

"Thirty years from now, the kids will be getting ready for Super Bowl LXI and NFL films will talk about how Brett Favre fought through such adversity.

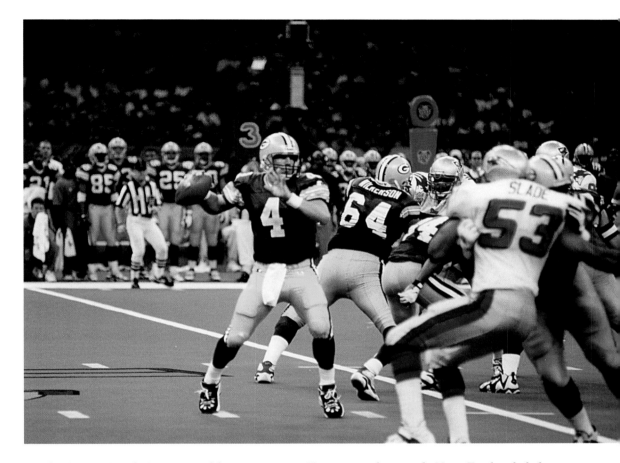

In the Super Bowl, Brett was like a surgeon. He cut up the tough New England defense with clutch passes in Green Bay's 35–21 victory.

There will be other players and coaches then. But I know this: We etched our place in history today."

Brett was right. His life hadn't all been easy despite being a gifted athlete. And he knows that it takes work to keep it on track. In 1996, Brett married his long-

Brett and Packers defensive end Reggie White celebrate the team's Super Bowl triumph together. A year earlier, Brett had promised White that he would lead the club to the title.

time sweetheart, Deanna Tynes. And after working so hard to reach the top of his profession, Brett has begun giving back.

In 1995 he raised more than $80,000 for the Boys and Girls Club of Green Bay by donating $150 for each of his touchdown passes and rushing touchdowns. He also arranged matching corporate contributions, and continues to do so. In February 1996, he started the Brett Favre Foundation with three youth-oriented charities reaping the benefits. They are the Special Olympics, Cystic Fibrosis, and the Boys and Girls Club.

He also hosts the annual Brett Favre Celebrity Golf Outing, with proceeds going to his foundation. In addition, Brett devotes his time to the Punt, Pass, and

Just a month after leading the Packers to the championship, Brett was back helping others. Here, he high-fives a young fan during a charity appearance on behalf of the Children's Hospital of Wisconsin.

Kick competition for kids and acts as a commercial spokesman for a number of products.

It's a full life now, but one that Brett knows can come tumbling down quickly. It hasn't always been easy being Brett Favre, but his toughness and strong will have always prevailed and should continue to do so in the future.

BRETT FAVRE: HIGHLIGHTS

1969 Born on October 10 in Gulfport, Mississippi.

1982 As eighth grader, becomes starting third baseman on Hancock North Central High School baseball team.

1987 Sets school record by passing for 14 touchdowns as a freshman at University of Southern Mississippi.

1988 Leads Golden Eagles to 9–2 record and victory in Independence Bowl.

1990 Recovers from car accident and intestinal surgery to lead Southern Mississippi to upset victories against Alabama and Auburn.
Named Most Valuable Player in East-West Shrine game.

1991 Picked by Atlanta Falcons in the second round of the NFL draft.

1992 Traded to Green Bay Packers. In third game of the season, completes 22 of 39 passes for 289 yards, and is named starting quarterback. Finishes season with 3,227 yards and 18 touchdowns. Packers, at 9–7, post their best record in twenty years. Favre becomes youngest quarterback to ever play in Pro Bowl.

1993 Throws for 3,303 yards and 19 touchdowns. Packs lose to Dallas Cowboys in second round of play-offs.

1994 Completes 363 of 582 passes for 3,882 yards and a team record 33 touchdowns. Green Bay finishes with 9–7 record for third consecutive season, losing again to Dallas in the play-offs.

1995 Throws a 99-yard touchdown against Chicago in game two.
Returns from injury to throw five touchdown passes in game ten.
Throws 100th career touchdown pass in only his sixty-second game.
Completes 359 of 570 passes for league-leading 4,413 yards and 38 touchdowns.
Named starting quarterback for NFC in Pro Bowl.
Named NFL Most Valuable Player.
Packers finish at 11–5, then lose to Dallas in the play-offs for third straight year.

1996 Completes 325 of 543 passes for 3,899 yards and 39 touchdowns.
Becomes only second player to win two consecutive NFL MVP Awards.
Green Bay posts 13–3 regular-season record, then defeats San Francisco and Carolina to win NFC title.

1997 Packers beat New England Patriots, 35–21, to win Super Bowl XXXI.

FIND OUT MORE

Gutman, Bill. *Football*. North Bellmore, NY: Marshall Cavendish, 1990.

Lace, William W. *Top Ten Football Quarterbacks*. Springfield, NJ: Enslow, 1994.

Mooney, Martin. *Brett Favre*. New York: Chelsea House, 1997.

Ryan, Pat. *Green Bay Packers*. Mankato, MN: Creative Education, 1991.

Wukovits, John. *Vince Lombardi*. New York: Chelsea House, 1997.

How to write to Brett Favre:

Brett Favre
c/o Green Bay Packers
1265 Lombardi Avenue
Green Bay, Wisconsin 54307-0628

INDEX

DATE DUE

JAN 2 8 2002			
FEB 0 7 2006			
FEB 1 3 2009			